Departure Dialogues:
Praying Like Jesus Prayed
as He Faced Death

By Debra Gustafson

MISSIONAL PRESS
-NASHVILLE, TN-

© 2021, by Debra Gustafson

ISBN: 978-1-7362821-3-7

All rights reserved. No part of this publication may be reproduced, distributed, or transmitted in any form or by any means, including photocopying, recording, or other electronic or mechanical methods, without the prior written permission of the publisher, except in the case of brief quotations in critical reviews and certain other noncommercial uses permitted by copyright law.

Scripture quotations taken from the ESV® Bible (The Holy Bible, English Standard Version®). Copyright 2001 by Crossway, a publishing ministry of Good News Publishers. All rights reserved.

Cover design by Katie Shull.

Published by:
Missional Press, a subsidiary of 610Media.
Nashville, TN
missionalpressbooks.com

Printed in the United States of America.

Departure Dialogues:

Praying Like Jesus Prayed as He Faced Death

By Debra Gustafson

Table of Contents for Departure Dialogues

Introduction……………………………………1
Listening Prayer……………………………..3
Luke 9:28-36
Lament…………………………………………..10
Matthew 23:37–39; Luke 13:34, 35
Prayer-Directed Action…………………….22
John 13
Intercession…………………………………...29
Luke 22:31, 32; John 17
Support Request……………………………36
Mark 14:32–34
Submission……………………………...……40
Mark 14:35, 36
Provision……………………………………….43
John 19:26, 27
Forgiveness……………………………………46
Luke 23:34
Salvation……………………………………….55
Luke 23:32–43
Surrender………………………………………59
Luke 23:46

Introduction to Departure Prayers
Learning from Jesus

Jesus was terminal. He knew in advance he would physically die. He knew it would involve suffering. Jesus talked to His Heavenly Father as He approached and entered His dying process. His closest friends heard and passed on His prayers. There are ten different prayer forms Jesus used that I present in this writing. These are available for us to use.

We know we will physically die. Some of us will have time to prepare for death due to medical diagnosis or advancing years. This short book briefly introduces us to Jesus' prayers and invites us to consider ways we can follow Jesus' examples.

The design of this writing is intentionally short, reflective, and invitational. Short: because persons approaching their active dying process generally do not read long writings or books. Reflective: a brief reflection of each prayer Jesus used is provided with examples of dying persons using a similar prayer. Invitational: an invitation is given for dying persons to write or draw their personal prayers in this book.

There are several benefits from following and learning from Jesus' departure prayers. They give us a model to follow. They provide words when we lack our own words in our journey. They invite us to feel close to Jesus. If needed, you can ask trusted family or friends to write or draw your prayers. Use this book alone or with others.

This book does not need to be followed chapter-by-chapter. Any reader can move through the prayer chapters however they choose. Not every prayer needs to be engaged with. Persons may wish to read and engage with the chapters which they discern applies to them. There is no correct way to proceed through this book; engage as you are prompted.

May this book be a blessing to you and those you love.

For the glory of God alone and your good,

Debra Gustafson
Ferndale, Washington
October 2021

Listening Prayer

I was working my high school summer job when I internally perceived the following message, "Go tell your grandmother the full message of My love!" The instruction came into my thoughts without warning and it held urgency.

I was working as a laborer on a residential construction site when the thought came. I tried to shake off the message by increasing the speed of my work. The urge to take immediate action associated with the message was persistent. I couldn't shake it, delete it, or explain it away. I was not prone to leaving a job responsibility in the middle of working hours, nor was I familiar with persistent urges bearing down or welling up in my soul. It was unrelenting, which made me entertain the thought that the message could be from God and the urgent nudging was the activity of the Holy Spirit.

Mustering courage, I asked my uncle for permission to leave for two hours, hoping he would not require my reason for leaving. Permission was granted with no explanation needed. In feeble prayer I drove to my grandmother's residence. Ruth McCauley had birthed 11 children, lived through the depression, and survived an alcoholic abusive husband who was a poor provider for their large family.

My grandmother had heard the gospel of Jesus Christ multiple times. It was not unfamiliar to her. For reasons unknown to me: perhaps disappointment, hopelessness, or her personal worldview, she had not responded to the offer of new and never-ending life in Jesus Christ. She did not personally know God's compassionate, saving love for her.

I sat with my alert and attentive grandmother as she lay in bed. There was nothing in the content of what I said that was new to my grandmother. What was certainly new to me was the expanding urgent compassion in my own emotion as I told her the message of God's love for us revealed in Jesus Christ. I spoke about Jesus' supreme sacrifice to offer people reconciliation with God. This was the Bible's salvation message, as I knew it at that time. Boldness, uncharacteristic to me, stirred inside and I said, "Grandma, I believe God has sent me here today to let you know it is time for you to make a decision about what He has done for us, for you, and what He promises those who trust Him. Will you respond in humility and begin a relationship with God?" To my surprise, large tears started leaking from my grandmother's eyes, rolling over the ridge of her nose and dropping on her pillow. In sympathy, I reached for a Kleenex on her bed stand, but internally perceived another unexpected message, "Don't move! She needs to make a spiritual move." I froze. Awareness settled over me that nothing was to interrupt my grandmother's free choice in that moment. I didn't move, but she did. She made the ultimate humble move of surrendering to the love of God through Christ Jesus. A long-standing hardened exterior fell off her soul through the drawing ministry of the Holy Spirit. She bowed her entire being and surrendered to Christ's love.

I called my mother, whom I knew had been praying for her mother's salvation for years. Mom came immediately. I left them and went back to work. They spent the evening together. For the first time, mother and daughter were sisters in Christ enjoying fellowship together. That night, my grandmother had a stroke that left her unable to communicate. Within a few days, she died and our pastor officiated her memorial service.

This was my beginning experience of learning to listen to God related to persons nearing their active dying process. The awareness that God cares for the dying profoundly captured my attention. A hunger began to grow in my soul to mature as a person willing to listen to God for the good of others and the world He deeply loves.

Jesus listened to His Father in prayer

Jesus was always listening to His Father. In John 5, Jesus spoke to those who were opposing his healing on the Sabbath:

"I tell you the truth, the Son can do nothing by himself; he can only do what he sees his father doing, because whatever the Father does the Son also does. For the Father loves the Son and shows him all he does." (vs. 19–20)

"By myself I can do nothing; I judge only as I hear, and my judgment is just, for I seek not to please myself but him who sent me." (v. 30)

Jesus was listening to His Father's voice and He obeyed what He heard. He listened and learned from God regarding His physical sufferings and dying. He spoke clearly with his closest followers about what was going to happen to Him (Mark 8:31; 10:32–34; 14:27–30; John 12:23–36; 14:1–4).

Learning to Listen to God

On the Mount of Transfiguration, God the Father was the voice in the cloud that spoke these words to Jesus' followers, Peter, James, and John: "This is my Son, whom I have chosen, listen to Him" (Luke 9:35).

Listen to Him!

Listening to God is one of the greatest helps available to every Christian (their family and loved ones) on their journey of physically dying. My niece uses essential oils. She has informed me from her study, Frankincense, is the king of all oils. I don't want to measure prayer forms against each other because all are important. However, could it be that listening prayer is foundational and the king of all prayers in people's dying process?

"Listen" literally means to "listen deeper than the ear." It is to listen in our souls with trust and obedience. All of life is an opportunity to keep maturing in learning to listen to God in prayer. Listening to God may be one of the greatest gifts we have in our active dying process.

For Reflection

Can you remember an experience when you heard God speaking to you in the past? You can record your thoughts in this space or share your experience with someone you trust.

Are you open to God speaking to you in your physical dying? What do you hear as you listen? Use the space below to write or draw what you hear. If you do not hear or perceive anything it is fine. You are fine.

Are there specific questions you have for Jesus/God?

My question for God is . . .

As I listen what I hear is . . .

As I engage further with God I perceive or hear . . .

Is there someone you would like to share what you believe you heard from God?

Lament

Stunning Loss

Norman was my childhood friend. We sat side-by-side on school buses, rushed our homework assignments and practiced our out-of-tune band instruments together. His trumpet and my saxophone made a horrible duet, but we called it "good enough" and quickly transitioned to creative outdoor adventures. We were avid fort-builders, bike-riders, berry-pickers, and explorers of all creatures living in the creek flowing between our homes. If we weren't in the water, we were climbing magnificent, tall fir trees lining "our creek." Our objective was to have fun and we did. The result was good friendship along with wet, dirty clothes. Shouts for dinner from parents or siblings stopped our creative play, but there was always the anticipation of tomorrow.

One violent windy, winter night while eating dinner, a distinct crash silenced our family table talk. Tires screeching, horns blowing and metal hitting metal pierced our peaceful dinner. Immediately Dad shoved his chair back and rose, giving one command, "Stay inside!" In silence, he tugged on his boots, snapped his work jacket and slipped out the side door into the howling wind. He had not returned by the time my Mom cajoled us kids to bed.

Dad was silent the next morning at breakfast. We asked for details about the loud crash. His Swedish reserve and inexperience expressing emotion kept him silent. This is common for many people including Bible reading Christians familiar with passages of scripture revealing, "Jesus wept in sorrow over Jerusalem (Matthew 23:37-39) or "cried out in a loud voice" from the cross (Mark 15:34). In silence, my Dad gathered his work coat and lunch pail. He stopped at our exterior door. Without facing us, he spoke. "Last night the entire VanDyke family died in a car accident at the end of our street. Debbie, I'm sorry about Norman." The door opened and Dad was gone.

I was stunned. My twelve-year-old heart skipped beats. An invisible fist slugged me in the stomach. Air escaped my lungs, but no sound came out. Mom instructed my brothers and me to get ready for school. Nothing else was said. Numb, I obeyed.

At the bus stop I saw the skid marks. Norman was not there. He would not sit beside me on the bus, or be in band class, or do homework or play together ever again. Norman was gone.

I was unable to articulate to another human the huge grief and anguished cry of lament stuck in my throat. At that time, I didn't have the gift or language of lament with which to tell others, "I can't sleep at night. I keep remembering the horrible sound of crashing metal and the stunning announcement Norman and his family were dead. I can't concentrate on schoolwork. I am completely shocked."

The Grief of Lament

Grief is the natural response to any loss we experience. Lament is the expression of the pain of our losses. Loss of a loved one, or a valued job, a treasured neighborhood community, physical mobility, or the losses associated with a worldwide pandemic, all become invitations to grieve. Loss can also be the absence of something we deeply desired to be a part of our lives but did not. Examples may be marriage, becoming a parent, having safety and security, or the hope to live near friends and family as we age. People experience loss in different ways. Sometimes we grieve what will never be as in a miscarriage or the death of a child or youth. Other times we grieve the loss of a long-term relationship, which is the grief of surrendering and letting go of what has been.

We remember and cherish but we grieve what will never be the same again in this physical realm. We grieve loss in different ways. No one-size fits all losses and personalities. Grief is not organized, nor does it progress the same way for all people or all situations.

What is lament, then? Lament is when we let our grief out. We may know we are lamenting or we may not fully understand what is cascading from our mouths, pens, souls, or hearts. We let out what is inside of us due to our loss. Letting grief out can be messy or it can be calculated and calm, but our grief comes out when we are lamenting. It may happen near the time of our loss or it can take years for our lament to be given expression. Delayed lament, due to shock, fear or lack of awareness, is just as deep and real as lament that is closer to the event(s) of our loss.

It is easy for some people to move away from God in their suffering and hurt, especially if we blame God for the hurt or loss. Prayers of lament keep us connected to God in our sufferings during life's disorientations and disappointments. A prayer of lament gives us a pathway of communication which we can use to remain healthy and whole in losses, including the death of our loved ones and in our own active dying process.

I was not given instruction regarding lamenting Norman's death. Nor was my dad. Years later, my Mother told me dad was the first person at the scene of the accident. The wind was so powerful, Norman's family's small Volkswagen car was thrust into the path of a large semi-truck. Norman's family of five were in the car. They all died. My Dad had his own lament. I had mine. But we did not know the language of lament.

The Language of Lament

A lament is an honest expression of how we feel about our loss, grief, sorrow, pain, confusion, betrayal, and disorientation, to name some examples. Christian lament is honest communication with God regarding our loss. It can be verbal, silent or written communication with God. It can be highly emotional and demonstrative or very quiet. Jesus used the language of lament in prayer with his heavenly Father. During emotional distress, physical pain and when entering his physical dying process Jesus let out his lament to his Father. In the New Testament book of Hebrews,

Chapter 5, we observe a summary of Jesus' healthy example of lament. It reveals:

"During the days of Jesus' life on earth, he offered up prayers and petitions with fervent cries and tears to the one who could save him from death, and he was heard because of his reverent submission. Son though he was, he learned obedience from what he suffered." (Hebrews 5:7,8)

Humanity was given a great gift in Jesus' use of lamenting prayer with His Father. God gives us freedom to pray our own gut-wrenching laments with cries, tears, and words while remaining close to Him who hears and promises never to leave us alone. Lament prayers allow a torrent of pain to cascade out of our souls and bodies, as we remain connected to a compassionate, listening God.

In His hour of need, upon the cross, Jesus could cry out in lament, "My God, My God, why have you forsaken me?" (Mark 15:34). This verse is a quote from Psalm 22. When Jesus cries out these words in a loud voice from the cross, does it mean He is angry and upset? Or is Jesus remaining relationally connected to God by using lament prayer? Luke 24:27 states that Jesus knew all the Scriptures concerning himself. "All" of Psalm 22 describes what He would experience. Jesus quotes only one verse, but the whole Psalm may have been on His mind. One of the horrors in crucifixion is that it becomes harder and harder for the victim to breathe. The sufferer is not likely to quote long passages from the Bible.

I believe Jesus knew all the verses in Psalm 22 and, it seems to me, in His dying process on the cross He is holding the whole prophetic Psalm in mind and soul. The progression in verses is listed below:

> "My God, My God, why have you forsaken me?" is the first verse of a Psalm that has thirty-one verses. The whole of Psalm 22 reveals a good pattern of prayer anyone could use in times of sorrow and lament.
>
> We cry out in our pain and our sufferings, sort of like "telling God what it really feels like."
>
> We ask for help from God. Crying out to God and asking for his help reveals trust and faith in God.
>
> We offer praise and adoration to God.
>
> We express hope for the future trusting God can and will provide for us in this life and the next.

You may consider reading all of Psalm 22 looking for the following transitions:

- ♦ Verse 1-2 is lament.

- Verses 6-8 and 12-18 express how bad the sufferer feels and how wrong the situation is.
- Verses 19–21 requests God's help.
- Verses 22-26 offer praise and adoration.
- Verses 27–31 express hope for the future.

With prayers of lament, we start out with our distress and agony expressed to God in our own words or we can use Jesus' words: "My God, My God why have you forsaken me? Why are you so far from saving me, so far from the cries of my anguish?"

As we progress in our lament, we can move to requesting help, to praising God and to exhibiting hope for self and others.

Prayers of lament can be used individually or corporately. I was in Chicago serving in an urban church when the terrorist attacks on America involving hijacked US planes crashing into the Twin Towers and the Pentagon. As I watched the planes plunge into the towers and witnessed the sufferings of humanity, I knew our church service the following Sunday would not be a normal service. We needed a worship experience that included corporate lament. Together we lamented for our fellow citizens deeply stunned, hurt and cast into grief and emotional sufferings. Months later, people were still reporting to me how valuable that corporate worship experience was to them.

For Reflection

Describe the events, relationship(s) or situation(s) you lament:

How might you express your personal lament? (Would it be in words, pictures, or poetry? Can you share this with God and/or others?)

What request do you have of God?

How would you offer praise to God?

How would you express your hope in the future?

Writing Invitation

When I layout my lament to God, I write . . .

When I listen to God, I hear . . .

I respond to God with . . .

When I further listen, I hear . . .

Examples of Lament in the Psalms

Psalm 13 is a lament of King David's.

How long, Lord? Will you forget me forever? How long will you hide your face from me? How long must I wrestle with my thoughts and day after day have sorrow in my heart? How long will my enemy triumph over me? Look on me and answer, Lord my God. Give light to my eyes, or I will sleep in death, and my enemy will say, "I have overcome him, and my foes will rejoice when I fall. But I trust in your unfailing love; my heart rejoices in your salvation. I will sing the Lord's praise, for he has been good to me. (vs. 1–6)

Biblical individual laments are found in Psalms 13, 18, 22, 32, 40, 42, and 51.
Communal laments are found in Psalms 44, 60, 74, 79, 80, 85, and 90.

PRAYER-DIRECTED ACTION
(or Prayer Informed Action)

Samuel knew he would soon die leaving his wife, six adult children and several grandchildren behind. Medical doctors and multiple tests confirmed it. Knowing in advance liberated Samuel to intentionally ponder caring for his family's emotional, mental, and spiritual wellbeing through and after his dying process. How would he say "Goodbye for now" to those he loved?

Samuel invited ten trusted friends and colleagues to regularly meet with him and his wife to discuss his desires. Together they designed avenues enabling Samuel to provide *prayer-directed actions* for his loved ones. He created individual memories for each loved one and constructed corporate memories they shared as a family. The team of ten became the helping hands Samuel needed to achieve his objectives. They faithfully fulfilled Samuel's requests and remained supportive of his relatives after his death.

Jesus knew He was approaching His death. He intentionally employed *prayer-directed action* as He knelt on the ground in a servant's posture before each of His chosen Apostles (John 13:1-17). The role involved washing the dirt and mud from bare or sandaled feet traveling dusty roads and pathways. Wiping each foot with a towel was an act of love flowing from a leader to His followers. In Jesus' day slaves or hired servants washed feet, not rabbis or the One these twelve men called Lord. Jesus' posture of prayer—directed actions by touching, washing, cleansing, and drying wet feet, deeply struck the hearts and wills of the recipients.

"It was just before the Passover Festival. Jesus knew that the hour had come for him to leave this world and go to the Father. Having loved his own who were in the world, he loved them to the end. The evening meal was in progress, and the devil had already prompted Judas, the son of Simon Iscariot, to betray Jesus. Jesus knew that the Father had put all things under his power, and that he had come from God and was returning to God; so he got up from the meal, took off his outer clothing, and wrapped a towel around his waist. After that, he poured water into a basin and began to wash his disciples' feet, drying them with the towel that was wrapped around him. He came to Simon Peter, who said to him, 'Lord, are you going to wash my feet?' Jesus replied, 'You do not realize now what I am doing, but later you will understand.'

"When he had finished washing their feet, Jesus put on his clothes and returned to his place. 'Do you understand what I have done for you?' he asked them. 'You call me "Teacher" and "Lord," and rightly so, for that is what I am. Now that I, your Lord and Teacher, have washed your feet, you also should wash one another's feet. I have set you an example that you should do as I have done for you. Very truly I tell you, no servant is greater than his master, nor is a messenger greater than the one who sent him. Now that you know these things, you will be blessed if you do them.'" (John 13:1-17)

Jesus was modeling prayer-directed action to His beloved Apostles. No one was overlooked; all were served. Was Jesus calling them and us to pray via our actions of service and sacrifice? Was He inviting them to use their entire bodies and hearts, to lay aside any distinguishing cloths or titles that identified them as anyone but a servant using *prayer-directed action*?

Samuel offered words, actions, and gifts that expressed his love and hope for each family member. Below are examples of the corporate discernment that surfaced out of prayer and discussions with his wife and the ten friends they invited to share the present and ongoing journey with Samuel's family after his death.

First, He met individually with each loved one speaking words of love, affirmation and blessing appropriate to his fatherly and husband knowledge. He gave gifts of high value he prayerfully picked for each person. For some it was a memorable adventure alone with their father. For others it was a material gift he knew his child would cherish for years to come.

Then, He held family gatherings where he prepared specific memories and facilitated space for them to share their common history, vacations, pictures, journals, etc. They shared future hopes with laughter and tears.

He also periodically met with the team of ten and the whole family affirming their desire and commitment to be supportive after Samuel's death. The family already had relationship with many of the ten. Gathering together increased trust and vulnerability, fostering deeper growth in their relationships.

Fourth, the team of ten knew a twenty-year-old personal desire Samuel held. He yearned for a few dear friends to ride motorcycles with him, meandering down one side of the winding Mississippi River and return the opposite side. He envisioned tenting and sharing life stories around evening campfires. Personal stories of any sort were a treasure to Samuel when all were free to share them in trusted community.

The team of ten knew Samuel wanted a bike "with a story." They also knew Samuel had been my pastor for fifteen years. He confirmed me, baptized me, and allowed me to preach my first sermon without any seminary education. He recruited me to join his adventurous aspiration of touring motorcycles beside the meandering river sharing life memories and lessons. The team of ten called me and requested to purchase my motorcycle knowing Samuel had been a spiritual mentor to me. I freely gave my Honda Hawk 750cc at their request, but they insisted on paying. They would not give Samuel a gift that cost them nothing. Their aim was to move him closer to his personal dream prior to his death. These ten were also *praying with action*!

Time was shorter than Samuel knew. He enjoyed the motorcycle riding but never got to experience his

Mississippi River dream. He did fulfill his desire to *pray directed action* over loved ones individually and collectively.

Lastly, the family planned Samuel's memorial service with him. The ten helped host and greet at the service freeing the family to be present with each other and guests.

For Reflection

Do you have a group of trusted friends to help you with your present and future prayer-directed actions to your loved ones? Who would you invite to join you in expressing your love and care to each person?

Who do you wish to express your prayer-directed loving action to? Would you like to give them a gift? Or write or speak words of love and value to them? What are your ideas?

How might you *pray in action* that is consistent with your character and your love and knowledge of each person(s)?

What ways would you value Jesus and others expressing their love in action to you? Can you ask for what you desire?

Intersession

"Cancerous tumors are aggressively growing in the bottom of both your lungs Pete." This was the doctors stunning sentence when my dad failed to fight off a winter cold leading to lung x-rays and biopsies. "Approximately twelve months to live." It was a death sentence he never expected or wanted.

My dad worked in the trades to provide for his family. As a self-taught nurseryman, his dream was to live many years after retirement nurturing flowers, trees, and shrubs. Construction debris silently wedged between lung cells, erupting into tumors crushed his retirement hope.

The congregation I served in Chicago granted me a thirty-day leave to spend time with dad before he descended deeply into his decline. When I arrived, I learned he could no longer lie flat at night. Back pain hindered his sleep. A recliner in the living room became his bed.

My first night home, I fell into bed drifting toward sleep when I heard a terrifying sound. The noise jerked me fully awake. It sounded like a cat trying to cough up a fur ball lodged in its throat. Instantly I thought, 'Dad is having a heart attack!' I bounded to his side.

My dad sat in his chair awake, trying to cry. A tissue dangled in his hand, but no tears fell to wipe away. He was inexperienced with crying. When it was time to cry and grieve, he could not. He wanted to. He needed to. But tears or sobs would not come. My emotions for him stuck in my throat as well. As my father's daughter, I didn't know how to move forward into tears of release either.

I knelt beside dad, gently holding him the best I could, desperately trying not to cause physical pain. He spoke first. "Oh Debbie, I'm just having a pity party. Please pray for me!" People in self-pity usually do not ask for God's help or request others to intercede for them in Jesus' name. Dad may have been inexperienced with crying, but he was experienced with prayers of intercession to God.

Jesus wanted His closest friends to pray for Him in His darkest hours of need. In Mark 14:32-34 Jesus shared with Peter, James, and John that His soul was overwhelmed to the point of death. He asked them to stay awake and pray while He poured out His own intercession to His heavenly Father. Prayer does not need to be a solely private experience. It can be. We can also ask trusted friends and family to pray for us in times of deep vulnerability as when we stare physical death in the face.

If you could make one request of Jesus to teach you something you witnessed in His life, what would it be? It fascinates me that Jesus' immediate followers asked him, "Teach us to pray" (Matthew 6:8). They did not ask, "Lord, teach us to heal the sick or cast out demons." Jesus did teach them to minister in these ways through

His name and authority. But having observed Jesus' life, what they requested of Jesus was, "Teach us how to pray, Jesus." They knew Jesus' prayer life with His Heavenly Father was critical to His daily life on earth. It guided and nurtured Him. It allowed love and power to flow through Him to others. They wanted to learn from Jesus how to pray.

"Teach us to pray." He answered, "This, then, is how you should pray: "Our Father in heaven, hallowed be your name, your kingdom come, your will be done, on earth as it is in heaven. Give us today our daily bread. And forgive us our debts, as we also have forgiven our debtors. And lead us not into temptation, but deliver us from the evil one." (Matt 6: 9-13; Luke 11:2-4)

In the New Testament book of Hebrews there is a reference to Jesus being an example of interceding to God the Father. It reveals:

"During the days of Jesus' life on earth, he offered up prayers and petitions with fervent cries and tears to the one who could save him from death, and he was heard because of his reverent submission. Son though he was, he learned obedience from what he suffered." (Hebrews 5:7-9)

Jesus learned to intercede with tears and cries and requests as He poured out His heart to His Heavenly Father. In His hour of need, heading toward the cross and His painful death, Jesus pressed into interceding to God in prayer.

Reflection

Would you like to be prayed for by other Christians? Who would you like to ask to pray with and for you? Can someone help you arrange this if needed?

Who is on your heart to intercede for? You may even consider praying for them in person or writing or recording your prayer for them to receive later.

Another example of Jesus' intercessory prayer life is found in John 17. I have chosen to include verses 9–23 for your personal consideration, but you can also read all of John 17 if you wish.

"I pray for them. I am not praying for the world, but for those you have given me, for they are yours. All I have is yours, and all you have is mine. And glory has come to me through them. I will remain in the world no longer, but they are still in the world, and I am coming to you. Holy Father, protect them by the power of your name, the name you gave me, so that they may be one as we are one. While I was with them, I protected them and kept them safe by that name you gave me. None has been lost except the one doomed to destruction so that Scripture would be fulfilled. I am coming to you now, but I say these things while I am still in the world, so that they may have the full measure of my joy within them. I have given them your word and the world has hated them, for they are not of the world any more than I am of the world. My prayer is not that you take them out of the world but that you protect them from the evil one. They are not of the world, even as I am not of it. Sanctify them by the truth; your word is truth. As you sent me into the world, I have sent them into the world. For them I sanctify myself, that they too may be truly sanctified."

Jesus not only prayed for His disciples, He prays for all believers.

"My prayer is not for them alone. I pray also for those who will believe in me through their message, that all of them may be one, Father, just as you are in me and I am in you. May they also be in us so that the world may believe that you have sent me. I have given them the glory that you gave me, that they may be one as we are one. I in them and you in me—so that they may be brought to complete unity. Then the world will know that you sent me and have loved them even as you have loved me."

Romans 8:34b reveals Jesus is interceding for us now: "Jesus Christ, who died–more than that, who was raised to life–is at the right hand of God and is also interceding for us."

Many Christians are comforted by the truth of Jesus interceding for us now in our daily lives and in all our seasons of life. My Dad wanted me to intercede to God for him as he neared his death. I was honored to gently hold him and pray in Jesus' name for his needs, comfort, and faith related to whatever he would face in the days to come. I also believed Jesus was interceding for my Dad and myself as I gently held him and prayed.

Remember you are prayed for by Jesus. This is true throughout your whole life. It is true in your aging and vulnerability. It is true if you are the loved one of someone who is in decline and dying.

Reflection

What would you like to ask Jesus to intercede for you?

Support Request

The loving middle-aged couple met me in my office to discuss the impending death of the wife's mother. The mother had been a long-time member of the church I was serving. Her declining health had prevented her from coming to church for several months. She sent her daughter and son-in-law to ask me if I could be called day or night as she neared her final breaths. She requested through them that I be there to pray with and for her. She wanted her pastor's support.

It was an honor to be asked. I had regularly been visiting Viola and served her Holy Communion monthly. But she had a deeper request on her heart. Perhaps it was one she did not feel comfortable asking me herself. My answer to the couple was a reassuring "Yes, day or night, I will come and pray and remain through her transfer to glory."

In the days ahead of her growing closer to her departure, she shared with me several prayer requests she held in her heart for those she loved and for herself. Some days she allowed me to see her deep emotional distress with tears and few words. Other days, she mostly talked or listened as I read Scripture to her and prayed. I was thankful for every visit. My compassion increased for her and her years of engagement in Grace Church.

I got the call in the middle of the night to come to her side as her family felt her departure was nearing. I dressed and entered their home with a prayerful heart. I was praying out loud and silently for only twenty minutes prior to her peaceful passing.

This precious saint could share her troubled heart with me and request that I pray with her and for her. Whether she knew it or not she was doing exactly what Jesus did with Peter, James, and John.

They went to a place called Gethsemane, and Jesus said to his disciples, "Sit here while I pray." He took Peter, James and John along with him, and he began to be deeply distressed and troubled. "My soul is overwhelmed with sorrow to the point of death," he said to them. "Stay here and keep watch." (Mark 13:32–34, NIV)

Reflection

As you face death, who would you like to be with you? How will you ask them for what you desire?

What emotions would you like to express to God and/or others about your dying and death?

Is there heaviness or sorrow in your heart you would like prayer for?

How would you like them to pray for you now?

How would you like them to "keep watch" with you as you transfer to Jesus?

More of the Biblical text can be found in Mark 14:32-42.

Submission

Beth did not want to die. She was the mother of three young children. Her doctors gravely reported that she had Hodgkin's lymphoma and it was terminal. Beth and her family deeply wanted this cup of death to pass from her. She wanted to live! Though her diagnosis was advanced, with her husband's help they tried different drugs granting her eleven months of remission. Then the disease struck back quickly. They flew to Mexico and tried drugs one could only get there. They hoped it would stop cancer growth. Nothing worked. They tried everything available to them including multiple church prayer meetings for Beth's healing by God. Beth's husband Kyle was the pastor of our church.

Though Beth did not want to die, leaving her children motherless, she and her husband began to surrender to death's reality. As a friend of the family and frequent babysitter for their children, I was granted an inside view of how Beth cooperated with Jesus regarding her impending death. She meditated and prayed repeatedly through Mark 14:35–36: "Going a little further, Jesus fell to the ground and prayed that if were possible the hour might pass from him. 'Abba, Father,' he said, 'everything is possible for you. Take this cup from me. Yet, not what I will, but what you will.'"

Jesus was choosing to submit to His Father's will more than His personal longing not to drink a cup of great suffering. Beth was choosing to submit to God's plans related to her dying and those she would leave behind. There were many tears and prayers and Beth recorded messages for each child to have after she died.

The Biblical account of how Jesus submitted to His Father is a help for all who know in advance we will face physical death. This can help all, since we will all physically die.

Reflection

What is the authentic cry of your heart to God at this time?

Can you ask God for help to pray like Jesus, "Not what I will, but what you will?"

What steps can you take now, like leaving recorded or written messages for your loved ones, that will help you submit to physical death?

Provision

"When Jesus saw his mother there, and the disciple whom he loved standing nearby, he said to her, 'Woman, here is your son' and to the disciple, 'Here is your mother.' From that time on, this disciple took her into his home." (John 19:26, 27)

God provides for us. Jesus' death and resurrection are God's gracious provision for us.

Scripture also reveals to us His concern and care of his earthly mother. In His dying on the cross Jesus chose John, a beloved follower, to become Mary's care provider. History reveals John did what Jesus requested. Jesus chose someone who believed in Him and was relationally close to Him. We can believe Mary lived the rest of her days on earth with John and not with her biological children. Sometimes the family of God may be closer to us than our own biological family.

Sarah was single. She had never married. She was deeply befriended by a family in her church. They grew so close, the family had her come live in an attached apartment to their home. They became like family over the years. Sarah celebrated all holidays with the family who had adopted her and treated her as a beloved member. Upon the husband's retirement, they had a new house built in the state they originally came from. Their love for Sarah was so close they asked her if she wanted to continue living beside them. With great joy Sarah said yes. She was allowed to work with the architect on her attached unit to the family that had claimed her as their own.

Even in Jesus' agony and suffering on the cross He was thinking of His mother's ongoing care. He asked His disciple John if he would care for Mary as he would his own mother. John did.

Reflection

Have you previously written down your Memorial Service and end of life desires and given them to your family or those closest to you?

Are there any provisions for yourself in your dying you would like to ask for at this time or remind your caregivers of?

What are the questions your caregivers have for you at this time related to your dying and the care of your body after death?

Forgiveness

It is common for persons in the active dying process to experience their capacities and spheres of influence diminishing. Engagement in the wider world grows smaller and narrower. This is natural. People seek to conserve energy. They may become quieter and disengage from activities or conversations once readily enjoyed. We also know dementia may be present as we decline.

Jesus had the capacity to stay fully engaged in His active dying process. While physically and emotionally suffering crucifixion, He becomes humanity's *sin bearer*. Jesus had remarkable maturity to stay present and outward focused while dying. He remained in prayer with His Father. He was concerned for persons around Him and all of creation. This is evident in His words from the cross, "Father, forgive them, for they do not know what they are doing" (Luke 23:34a).

Lori came to our church's Alpha Course in 2004. Her life journey had been difficult and challenging. She was raising two teenage daughters who had little interest in learning life skills, being in school, or respecting their mother. The three of them were living in a tiny subsidized apartment in urban Chicago when I was introduced to them.

What I didn't know the first time I met Lori was she was dying of cervical cancer. It was rapidly spreading to her other organs. She already had a colostomy. Through her Alpha Course involvement Lori became a Christian and was mentored weekly in Bible study and prayer by her leaders. Our church became intimately involved in caring for Lori and her daughters. Clothing, furniture, money, prayer times, Bible studies, listening, staying overnight, and offers of transportation were graciously provided for them.

Lori lapped up the Alpha Course and Bible studies like a thirsty, dehydrated, desert wanderer. She welcomed the love, forgiveness, and Lordship of Jesus Christ into her life. She transferred from darkness to light through placing her faith in Jesus Christ.

As Lori matured in her learning to follow Jesus Christ, she led her two daughters into a living relationship with Him. When I baptized the three of them in a Sunday morning worship service it was a day of great rejoicing in our church community.

Lori delighted to be folded into the church family. This continued until her health declined and she was admitted into a hospice care facility. Hospice personnel were marvelous to her and so was the church community. Several women stayed nights so Lori would not be alone. Others sat with her in the day times.

I witnessed God's loving guidance and growth in Lori. Four days before Lori's physical death I was praying for her early in the morning. An image of her came into my mind's eye: I saw Lori standing in a warrior-like poise, dressed in heavy, thick armor. The armor protected her from head to foot. She held a sword in her hand in an attacking posture. In prayer I asked, "What is this Lord?" Then the image completely changed. The armor was gone, and I saw Jesus dressing Lori in a beautiful bright-white wedding dress. Listening for the Lord's instruction I asked, "Oh Lord, please show me what you are doing and what you desire me to say or do to assist Lori." The second image went away. No words from the Lord accompanied the pictures yet I knew it was the activity of God. I was grateful I was visiting Lori that afternoon.

When I arrived at her hospice room, Lori was physically weak, but she was coherent, completely present and enjoying talking with Sue who was staying with her. We chatted a while, then I asked if we could pray. Lori liked when church people prayed with her or sang to her. Like a dry sponge Lori lapped up people's love and God's living water. After invoking the Lord's loving presence to be with us, I sensed that it might be good to tell Lori the first picture I saw and then invited her to listen to the Lord in prayer. Sue was deeply intrigued while I described to Lori the picture of her dressed from head to foot with the sword in the attack posture. Lori had her eyes closed but when she heard the scene described, she spontaneously laughed out loud and opened her eyes in awe. I was surprised by Lori's response.

When I asked Lori why she laughed, she exclaimed that the picture was a perfect illustration of how she lived her life. She described the heavy armor as her life-long self-protection and the sword as her weapon if she needed to defend herself or daughters from harm. As I listened, I was silently asking the Lord, "Now what?" A bold gentleness came over me and I asked Lori if we could keep praying.

She was totally present and quite taken with the picture that connected clearly with her life. As we listened for Jesus' leadership, I said, "Lori, where you are going you do not need any armor to protect you. There will be no need for you to defend yourself or attack others." Lori's face looked shocked. I continued, "I want to ask you an important question? Are you willing to let Jesus take the armor off of you, piece by piece?" After some deep authentic thought, Lori yielded with a genuine, "Yes!" I invited her to perceive the Lord Jesus with her as she stood dressed in the weighty armor. It was armor she collected in response to being hurt and deceived in her fifty years of life. And I suspect the armor was representative of her hurting others. After several minutes she revealed she could perceive the Lord with her. Then I said, "Lori, can Jesus have your armor? Can He have your helmet? Where you are going, no one will mess with your mind again. There will be no more deception, manipulation, game playing, second-guessing, self-doubt or the swirl of trying to figure out other people's motives. It will be clear and it will be clean. Can Jesus have your helmet?" Lori opened her eyes and gazed into mine. They were questioning eyes as if asking, "Pastor Deb, do you promise this is true?" Just reading her face and understanding she did not know the Bible well, I assured her the Bible revealed that life in Jesus' full Kingdom realm will be devoid of all deception and mental games.

She closed her eyes again and said, "Jesus, will you take off my helmet. I guess I won't be needing it anymore." After several long seconds she reported He took it from her and laid it at His feet. Praying in this fashion over the following thirty minutes with assurance from Scripture and Jesus, Lori surrendered all her self-protective armor to her Lord and Savior. She also surrendered the sword in her hand. She described it as all lying at the feet of Jesus. She said she could still perceive Jesus in front of her and He seemed pleased with her trust.

I asked Jesus what He wanted next. In listening for His leadership, the thought came to me of David who wrote in Psalm 139:23b, "Search me, God, and know my heart." I surely did not know what unconfessed sin might still be in Lori's heart from her sojourn through life. I described David's prayer and asked Lori if I could invite Jesus to search throughout her body, mind, memories, history, and experiences to see if there was anything else, He would invite her to lay at His feet in surrender. My hope was that everything would be brought under Jesus Christ's authority in this realm before Lori went into her active dying process. Lori assured me the type of prayer I described would be fine. I prayed and then waited. Within thirty seconds she said, "Oh boy, Pastor, there is something that came to my mind." I invited her to confess it to Jesus and let Him guide her from there. She insisted she was supposed to say it out loud.

She revealed she had had two abortions and she never asked God to forgive her. I invited her to pray in her own words and confess the sin of destroying life made in God's image. In earnest sincerity, Lori prayed her confession and requested forgiveness for what she had done. I then asked her if she could perceive Jesus' face. She quickly replied, "Yes." I asked if she perceived anger, disgust, or frustration from Jesus toward her. With her eyes still closed, a broad smile broke across her previously blank face. "Love; just love! He forgives me. He is not mad at me. He loves me and will soon introduce me to my children." Lori's face appeared to have a sweet glow upon it as she leaned on her pillow. She was definitely enjoying God's presence, grace, and forgiveness. I internally asked the Lord, "What do you want to do or say next?"

This is what transpired. I did not tell Lori about the second picture I had seen praying for her that morning, I asked her to be open to receiving whatever the Lord Jesus had for her. I was aware it would likely be something from Him that would be a replacement for the armor lying at His feet. With eyes closed Lori continued to focus her attention on Jesus. Within a short period of time, another broad and joyful smile swept across her thin face and she exclaimed, "It's beautiful, it is so beautiful!" Tears began dripping down her face. Sue had no idea what was transpiring and looked ready to ask

Lori a question. I gently motioned for her to wait. Then I quietly asked Lori, "Is it your size?" Immediately she said, "Yes, yes, it is my size and it is so white and beautiful." I asked her if Jesus could help her put it on. To my surprise Lori lifted her slender, bony arms in the air to receive the gift of the beautiful wedding dress she perceived Jesus was providing for her.

Sue looked dumbfounded but was hanging on every word and movement from Lori believing the Lord was at His work of love. I was in wonder and in tears as Lori basked in the love, forgiveness and new hope of what her Savior had for her in the present and in the future. It was a glorious hour of preparatory cleansing for Lori. It was also a time where her trust in the character and love of her Savior was strengthened.

God was glorified in that hour of prayer and Lori was being prepared for her departure from this realm through the gift of God's complete forgiveness. I have not been the same since witnessing the love and forgiveness of God toward this daughter who suffered and struggled to live in this sin-impacted world. Lori had never married. She had lived with lots of men. But this was the first wedding dress she had been given by the greatest Bridegroom the world has known.

Lori was cleansed from her sins, not keeping anything a secret. She transferred to the full presence of our Triune God four days later.

Having our sins cleaned up as we enter our active dying process is precious. It honors Jesus' complete sacrifice and His authority to forgive sin.

For Reflection

Are you willing to ask Jesus to reveal any sin in your life that needs to be confessed to God? Can you receive His forgiveness? Do you have someone you wish to be with you during this prayer time?

Is there some person, group or entity you need to extend forgiveness to? You can confess to God. You can extend forgiveness to others any time, day or night.

Jesus did not need to confess sin or ask forgiveness of His Father. He was sinless. He had the authority to forgive sin. But we may have persons or a group or an institution we need to forgive because they sinned against us. Can you follow Jesus' example of forgiving them? You may value using Jesus' words, "Father, forgive them, for they did not know what they were doing?"

Salvation

When I answered the phone there was an excited voice saying, "Come quickly Pastor, I feel a wind moving around me in my apartment." I asked Joseph whether it was a frightening or peaceful wind. He reported it was peaceful, but he did not know what it was. I quickly ran to Joseph's apartment a few blocks from the parsonage I lived in. I was the pastor of Joseph's father, but Joseph did not have anything to do with church.

We were acquittances. I saw Joseph often because of my relationship with his dad. At the time of Joseph's wind experience, his dad was in the hospital and was not expected to live more than a week, if that. When I arrived, Joseph sat on his couch deeply emotionally moved by the warm, kind, strange wind he felt moving around him. Joseph knew his dad was dying. He also knew one of his father's deepest hopes and prayer was that his beloved son would become a genuine follower of Christ. His dad and I regularly prayed for Joseph to experience God's love moving in his life. The gentle wind which deeply moved Joseph was capturing his attention related to there being a loving God from whom he might be willing to seek salvation.

Joseph and I talked about the places God revealed Himself in the Bible through a wind. He wanted to go visit his dad in the hospital and asked me to come. Upon our arrival, Russ was fully alert and oriented. With vast interest and smiles he listened to his son as Joseph relayed the warm, kind swirling wind around him. I was privileged to sit quietly as a dying father led his precious son into a living relationship with Jesus Christ. Even in Russ's pain, he made his son's salvation his priority.

Jesus Christ was crucified in the middle of two other men. Below is Luke's account of Jesus' crucifixion and the salvation account of one man crucified beside Him.

"Two other men, both criminals, were also led out with him to be executed. When they came to the place called the Skull, they crucified him there, along with the criminals—one on his right, the other on his left. Jesus said, 'Father, forgive them, for they do not know what they are doing.' And they divided up his clothes by casting lots. The people stood watching, and the rulers even sneered at him. They said, 'He saved others; let him save himself if he is God's Messiah, the Chosen One.' The soldiers also came up and mocked him. They offered him wine vinegar and said, 'If you are the king of the Jews, save yourself.' There was a written notice above him, which read: this is the king of the Jews. One of the criminals who hung there, hurled insults at him: 'Aren't you the Messiah? Save yourself and us!' But the other criminal rebuked him. 'Don't you fear God,' he said, 'since you are under the same sentence? We are punished justly, for we are getting what our deeds deserve. But this man has done nothing wrong.' Then he said, 'Jesus, remember me when you come into your kingdom.' Jesus answered him, 'Truly I tell you, today you will be with me in paradise.'" (Luke 23:32–43)

Reflection

Who do you desire to come into a living relationship with Jesus Christ?

What might you lovingly say or do or write to someone you wish to become a Christian?

Have you come into a living relationship with Jesus where you can, silently or out loud say, "I will soon be with Jesus Christ in His paradise?"

"Surrender"

In 1997 I was called to pastor a small urban church in Chicago. Church persons wanted me to meet the oldest and longest member of the congregation. Nina Larson was eighty-eight years-old and she had been in the church since she was in her mother's womb. The church itself was founded in 1898. Nina was the living history of the church community knowing the congregation and buildings better than any other person. She held every volunteer position in the church except Chairman of the Church Board. She also attended more funerals of people she loved than anyone I've known. She passed forward to Jesus' full realm after ninety-three years without changing churches or missing many Grace Church gatherings.

She out-lived her closest Christian friends, all of her believing family members, and her dearest confidantes. The temporary removal of these loved ones and all whom Nina had shared deepest fellowship with, was a loss to her. She knew she would see them again in the full Kingdom of God, but she felt the loss and grief of each passing Christian member and friend. She never married so her biological and church family were her closest community.

It was a pleasure and honor for me to be Nina's pastor. She was named Nina because she was the ninth child born into her large family. As she aged, I came to understand that Nina's largest vulnerability was not the loss of bodily functions, or strength and mobility; it was the reality that she was in the hands of relatives who did not share her faithful obedience to the God of the Bible. She had outlived her believing family. This meant during Nina's physical decline she was in the hands and decision processes of family who did not honor Jesus Christ, the Bible, or Christian ethics. This was Nina's greatest vulnerability and loss. She felt it keenly in the choice of the care facility chosen for her. She felt the lack of fellowship and prayer as her body declined. One illustration of her sorrow relates to hydration. When Nina's hands and arms began to greatly tremble and she was too weak to lift a water glass without spilling eighty percent of the fluid on herself and her bed, we at her church filled a backpack hiking hydration bladder with cold filtered water and attached the tube near Nina's head. All she needed to do for hydration was suck on the tube and drink. She was grateful.

Nina and I both felt her vulnerable plight on my visit the next day. To my surprise, the assembled drinking device was gone. A family member was present. The family member had removed the hydration bladder, drained its precious contents. When I entered Nina's room, the person forcefully handed me a sack saying quietly in my ear as she left the room, "Don't ever hook this up again! Do you have any idea how much it costs to keep her in this place? We are not going to prolong this one minute more!" In the sack was the drinking bladder, drained.

As Nina's pastor for six years, I grew to love and delight in her. I'm aware I felt only a small portion of Nina's lengthy vulnerability under the decision-making power of her pre-Christian relatives. At Nina's committal service a small number of her relatives were present. At her Memorial Service held in the church facility where she delighted to worship and loved every person, not one of her relatives attended. No family came to honor Nina where she had worshipped, served, loved, been loved, been taught and been respected for her entire life. It remains a painful lesson to me that there are many kinds of vulnerabilities that occur for the aging and ill.

Nina's physical death is one of the sweetest surrenders to God I have witnessed. It came on Sunday afternoon, March 2, 2003. It was as if Nina peacefully whispered to her God, "Into your hands I commit my spirit." There was no fear, no struggle, no seeking to cling to this life. I was with her when she transferred to Glory.

Right after our church service I invited two women I was mentoring to come with me to visit Nina. When we walked into Nina's room, an aide was feeding her some soup; no family was present. I cannot explain my next sentence except by the ministry of the Holy Spirit. The moment I walked into Nina's room and our eyes met, I knew in my spirit she was ready to depart her physical body and join her Master and Lord in a realm beyond this earthly realm. She was ready to participate with God. Silently we stood at the foot of her bed while the aide finished her work. I quietly told the two women with me that they were welcome to take my car and leave, but that I would be staying with Nina for an unknown period of time. The women wanted to stay with Nina for a while.

Nina had only one hearing ear, her left. She was partially sitting up in bed and her breathing was slightly labored, but she had no supplemental oxygen and no pain. Perhaps it is a benefit of being a woman clergy or perhaps it was the strength of relationship and trust Nina gave to me over the years and over the last months. When staff was too busy, she allowed me to change her soiled garments and wash her body. As I neared the head of her bed that Sunday, she took my hand and weakly pulled me toward her. I ended up half-sitting and half-lying beside her, cradling her head in my right arm. This gave me intimate access to her hearing left ear.

In this position my heart started to swell in love for Nina. I was able to thank her with tears for her faithful love for God and her faithful service to His church. I thanked her for helping keep the church going during hard years, during the language transition from Swedish to English. I affirmed that it was because of her and other's faithfulness that I now had the privilege of loving and serving in an urban church. With these thanksgivings and authentic honoring of her journey with Christ and the family of God, I felt Nina's body relax and lean into my arm and onto my body more and more.

The next thing that happened is usually the privilege of loving family at the right discerned moment, but in this case, God allowed it to be my privilege as pastor. I invited Nina to surrender fully to Christ and gave her permission to go to Him. I started to pray for her to hear the Lord Jesus call her name. Between my praying I was internally listening to the Lord for what he would have me pray or say next. I found my heart asking Christ, "What would you say to your daughter right now? How would you say it?" A host of hymns and Scriptures I knew were close to Nina's heart came flooding into my mind and soul. I started to quote her favorite Scripture which became her favorite Scripture simply because many, many years earlier a pastor wrote it in her confirmation Bible. "I have hidden your word in my heart that I might not sin against you" (Psalm 119:11). I quoted other passages she knew and loved. The women with me standing at the side of the bed wiping their own tears away, began to sing hymns. Between each hymn, I prayed what I felt God was giving me to pray for and over Nina. At one moment I found myself listening to the Lord and wondered if He whispered to my heart, "Command the darkness and dark shadows associated with death to stand aside and allow her to pass freely to Me." I removed my face from Nina's ear so she did not hear that prayer. This was new territory to me, and I was in an alert learning mode. By faith I prayed that all hindrance to her soul and personhood passing directly from this realm to the next would stand aside and not afflict her, torment her, or impede her passage to the resurrected Lord Jesus Christ. As we sang the next hymn, Nina's breathing dramatically changed. She was freely surrendering to the One who knew her and was calling her home. Into His hands she was committing her spirit.

I was gently saying brief messages in Nina's ear with silences in between the sentences, "Good job Nina!" "Keep listening for Jesus' voice!" "Keep surrendering to Him!" "Look for Jesus." "All the way your Savior leads you." "All the way Nina, go all the way to Jesus." Throughout this short time, I noticed slowed breathing, followed by a breath after thirty seconds. Nina took another inhalation after forty-five seconds. Silence. Then one last breath. All went still in Nina's body. Her hand stopped gripping mine. She was gone. I was holding, and we three were surrounding, Nina's earthly tent through which she knew and experienced the world.

Nina leaned into her Lord and surrendered her spirit to Him without struggle or fight. She had been fully conscious and coherent when we walked into her room. Within fifty-five minutes she was on her way to seeing Jesus face-to-face. I had anticipated it might take all night. I underestimated how ready and willing Nina was to commit herself into her faithful Savior's hands.

Nina had become dependent in her aging body. She had known loss and the pain of vulnerability at the end of her days. But on her final day, her faith was exceedingly ready to surrender to the One who called her and redeemed her. She followed the model Jesus gave us on the cross, when He said, "Father, into your hands, I commit my spirit!" It was an extremely sweet testimony of surrendered faith from a person who had become dependent, vulnerable and acquainted with loss. I praise God for Nina's model of living well and dying well. She trusted God and his Word. She is not disappointed.

Reflection

How will you surrender your soul in your dying moments? To whom will you surrender your soul?

Is there someone you would like to ask, in advance, if they can be with you when it is time to surrender your soul to God?